Shell Dreams

Ed Block

Water's Edge Press

Copyright © 2021 by Ed Block

All rights reserved.

Printed in the United States of America

Water's Edge Press LLC
Sheboygan, WI
watersedgepress.com

ISBN: 978-1-952526-07-7
Library of Congress Control Number: 2021945821

Credits

Cover photography by the author
Photo of the author by the author

A Water's Edge Press First Edition

Also by Ed Block

Anno Domini (Wipf & Stock, 2016)

Seasons of Change (Finishing Line Press, 2017)

Jon Hassler, Voice of the Heartland: A Critical Appraisal of his Work (Nodin Press, 2019)

To the memory of my late wife,
Mary Helen, who loved our time
on Sanibel.

Acknowledgements

Thanks to Dawn Hogue for invaluable artistic and editorial assistance.

The author is grateful to the editors of the following publications in which these poems first appeared, some in slightly different form:

Wisconsin Fellowship of Poets Triad Contest, "Florida Man"
Seasons of Change (Finishing Line Press), "A Map," "In the Keys With Maggie," "Duval Street," "On Key West"
Taj Mahal, "Anhinga"

Introduction

My wife and I spent five successive Februarys on Sanibel Island, located on the Gulf of Mexico and linked to Ft. Myers, Florida by a beautiful two-mile long causeway that pauses for half a mile or so in San Carlos Bay at Causeway Island Park.

The first year we rented a third floor condo at a large resort, but in subsequent years we stayed at a smaller resort, where we had a first floor condo whose lanai opened onto a lawn that led to the shell-strewn Gulf beach. We enjoyed fresh seafood, basked in the sun, and visited local attractions. We hunted shells and watched the sun go down each evening. "Island Time" meant no stress, no hurry. We only left the island occasionally to pick up visiting family members from the Ft. Myers airport. Once or twice each February, we drove north and then across the bridge over Blind Pass, which links Sanibel to Captiva Island. There we sampled the cuisine at different restaurants and watched para-sailers on the beach.

In each of the five years we drove a different route both going to and returning from our month in Florida, seeing as many sights along the way as time allowed.

Florida culture—as experienced on Sanibel—can induce a strange mix of indolence and self-absorption. While many visitors hail from colder northern states, most of the locals have been there for decades. The majority of workers on the island—wait staff, clerks, and maintenance people—commute across the causeway every morning, since they can't afford housing on Sanibel. The culture of the island is a mile wide and an inch deep. There are art galleries, a live theater, a library, and various civic organizations, but most visitors spend their time biking, playing golf, soaking in resort hot tubs, and drinking.

The poems in this short collection represent one poet's-eye view of some of the more fascinating aspects of life on Sanibel.

To Florida

- Flat as Kansas 1
- Above the Condos 2
- Awake at Moonrise 3
- Florida Pelicans 4
- Ocean Friends 5
- The Fog 6
- A Ship's Complaint 7
- Devil Bird 8
- Anhinga 9
- Florida Fantasy 10
- The Horseshoe Crab 11
- Florida Man 12
- Florida, Venereal Spoil 13
- In the Keys With Maggie 14
- Duval Street 15
- A Motel on Key West 16
- The sea, monstrous but restless 17
- On Key West 18

Sanibel

A Map 21
Shell-Seekers 22
This Island Is a State of Mind 23
February Sonnet 24
At the Club 25
On Sanibel 26
On Sanibel II 27
That Florida Feeling 28
Blind Pass 30
Pine Island / Another World 31
From Lover's Key 32
The South Side 33
The Lure of Sanibel 34

The Way North

A Theft in Charleston 37
The Old Shrimp Shack 38
An Apalachicola Suite 39
Apalachicola Impressions 40
Dollar Treed 41
Traveling North 42
Home 43

Behind the bougainvilleas,
After the guitar is asleep,
Lasciviously as the wind,
you come tormenting,
insatiable.

Wallace Stevens,
"O Florida, Venereal Soil"

Shell Dreams

Night winds change the Gulf beach
to an alien scape. Across the rippled sand
stretch yards and yards of shells cast up
from tropic deeps. The drills, the whelks
and tulips, their colors gray and pink
and ochre, striped, and spotted,
scattered remnants of a battle
with the sea;
                    and largest of them all,
the horse conch: turban-like, a dizzy spiral
ribbed and knobbed, striated,
an ancient visitor, its past
marked by its coat of barnacles.
A red-orange snail—its home
within the twisted whorls—
reigns supreme, almost majestic
over all the other stranded
shells thrown up to dry,
their occupants perhaps to die
before the tide returns
to claim its own and gather all
back to blue-green oblivion.

To Florida

Flat as Kansas

Flat as Kansas, but more humid;
ranged for cattle like
the intermountain West;
creeks and swamps
to match Louisiana,
coasts like California
and the Carolinas;
urban sprawl like in the Northeast
and the Midwest,

Florida, a contradiction.

Above the Condos

At night above the condos
strange constellations rise
where palm trees seek
to snare them. Waves
from the beach cast warnings
back to sky and stars.
In the parking lot hibiscus
release their scent and blossoms
onto paths and parked cars
their violent reds and docile pinks
now muted in the dark
but still a potent protest against
the everlasting ocean
and the distant stars.

Awake at Moonrise

all the world seems quiet.
Against a blackdrop
slowly the silver
sliver ascends in stillness
up the sky,
casting a sheen
on wide waters
until dove-
gray dawn rises
almost imperceptibly,
and with the fading
stars it disappears.

Florida Pelicans

No one, not even a poet, uses the word "pinions" anymore, in place of "wings." But watching pelicans, an observer might be at a loss to describe their effortless-seeming flight, a foot above the Gulf, or a foot above the palms; alone or in formations, muscular wings, and pinions beating powerfully, or swiftly folding as they dive into the surf for fish, causing an explosion or resembling a rock thrown from the shore. Black heads and bills poise motionless between dark shoulders and end feathers. But remember: down here they're as ubiquitous as Canada geese, the "sky rats" of the north.

Ocean Friends

The crows pretend they're seagulls
and the seagulls pretend
that they are pelicans. Birds
learn from one another;
how to hover, how to dive.
They brave the wind and rain
that toss and drench their feathers.
They share dead fish
and mollusk fragments, jelly-
fish, and thrive together.

The Fog

The fog takes the shape
of animals; a dolphin here,
a manatee; and there
a killer shark, farcically
fearsome yet delicate
and always changing.
Beneath the fog
the Gulf is quiet.
As the haze lifts,
slowly all the fog-birthed
animals will disappear.

A Ship's Complaint

I'm high and dry; my keel is cracked;
I haven't been surveyed. My rudder's off,
the tiller's jammed, my bilge is dry.
The sheets have all been frayed.
I need a paint job. Brightwork scarcely
glistens, yards need varnish, sails, a sew.

Over the shoals the ocean whispers as
it collapses into foam.
Again the water whispers:
"Kick out the chocks,
slide down the ways, and splash
like a great green turtle into the bight
that's blue as the sky and white with gulls.

"Put out, and make for the islands;
rum in plenty, bare buns. But beware.
The bums in sandals lurk. There
we'll find the Gulf Stream Muse
and woo her with drink
and coral necklaces;
tickle her with jokes
and gin fizz; make her
a drink she'll not forget,
and take her to bed
where the westerlies will lull us
to sleep in darkness, and only
blow aside the curtain
at a dawn as close to rosy-fingered as you need."

Devil Bird

Neck like a black snake, the anhinga
peeps its skinny head from just
above the surface like a water moccasin.
A gold stiletto beak and savage
stripes along its back inspire dread.
Neither "darter" nor "water turkey"
do justice to its evil appearance.

On shore it dries its wings; spread
out they look like a bat's. It cranes
and twists its neck and gives
a ghostly call. It dives for fish
like a missile, swimming
for yards submerged,
before that neck and beak again
appear, a terror to behold.

The word "anhinga" comes from the Brazilian Tupi language and means devil bird or snake bird. See the bird swimming and the origin of the name is clear; only the colored neck appears above water so the bird looks like a snake ready to strike.

Anhinga

I am the snakebird. You won't
see me underwater, until my narrow
head is on you in this southern swamp.
Stiletto-like, I spear my food
then dry my bat-like wings
while perching on a branch.
I fly high with outstretched wings
and tail. I look on the world
with blood-red eye. Beware,
you small fish, shrimp. Even
your baby alligator is my prey.

Florida Fantasy

Without a sound
the brown Casablanca
spins its fins
above the bed
cooling any passion
of the king
as it moves the humid
Gulf air through
the darkened room.

The shaded lamp
its patterned tint
casts dim mosaics
on the walls.

The closet and the dresser
drawers left open
and the shades awry,
the door and one dark
window left ajar, the stains
and scattered clothing
on the floor.
What came to pass here,
what Floridian mystery?

The fragments
of the broken mirror
reflect a scene
of chaos like the whirling notes
of a virtuoso troubadour.

The Horseshoe Crab

Homage to Ted Hughes

A crab shell on the beach;
seagull feathers, whelks, and drills,
and seaweed, tide-tossed, dry
then bleach back to the beginning of it all.

Restlessly the Gulf turns pages
of its history. With no love
or camaraderie, the waves say,
"What we serve up all was prey."

Time in the Gulf has no tale but:
"This achievement; shards and bones
ground fine." Disgorged, this crab,
these cuttlefish and banded tulips,
once thriving, now are one.

This horseshoe did not smile
but in death threw up its life
upon the Gulf shore pile.
In the depths it found that none
grow rich, but only die.
This crab gave up without a cry.

Florida Man

Florida Man goes dancing through my dreams
his antics more bizarre each day it seems.
He pops up everywhere, is he a ghost?
Or is he more than one? A parasite? A host?
He weaves along palm-haunted drives
and often ends up in the Tamiani dives.
He frequents Mar-a-Lago bars
and praises right-wing TV to the stars.
Florida Man defies the odds
by dancing on a knot of snakes unshod.
He drives his Porsche into a pond
then rises resurrected with a blonde
who clings to him with coy lordotic pose
in sheath and torn black fishnet hose.
Florida man develops scars
from dodging in and out
of wrong-way speeding cars.
Florida man ingests a lethal dose
of Lysol but survives to boast.
Florida man tells lies and claims they're truth
he is himself a hoax long in the tooth.
Florida Man's no figment of imagination
he's hailed as hero: one to save the nation.

Florida, Venereal Spoil

A backhanded tribute to Wallace Stevens

O, Florida, foreskin of America,
God's waiting room,
I celebrate your wild excesses.
From stinking swamp to gleaming high-rise,
Gulf coast fog to arid plain;
Stephen Foster, Tamiani, Apalachicola dreams.

The ghost of Henry Flagler haunts
the Keys and Everglades. The living ghosts
of politicians flaunt their wealth
in august Villages and dizzy worlds
and on Mar-a-Lago maids.

When rockets lift off, trapeze artists fall,
and sclerotic retirees relax,
while crazed commuters fly down freeways
plagued by wrong-way drivers high on speed,
we sing hosannas and our praise of sunshine's rays,
shell-hunters, and the thousand folks
each clever land developer betrays.

In the Keys With Maggie

Homage to Elizabeth Bishop

My place on Summerland,
        my prince's palace,
cozy as a clam; it's vinyl and aluminum
        a double-wide.
with A/C on the roof, a picture
        window on the sea.

This dump, my love-nest,
        sports bleached oak
for cabinets, a cast-
        iron fry pan in a stainless
tub. The laundry hangs
        outside; my girl-
friend, Maggie's bra and panties
        next to oilskins
that I wear
        when I go fishing
in the Gulf, for tarpon,
        oysters, razorbacks,
which seldom bite.

When I come home,
        we drink tequila,
jump in bed
        and don't wake up
until the morning light
        when we hear roosters
crow, or tourists
        on the causeway.
And better than the fish,
        my Maggie bites.

Duval Street

Down Duval, swept with the crowd
of visitors, to the shore. The cruise
ship towers over everything: the tourist trains,
the pirates, and the pretty maids
with tattooed legs and arms
who walk along, tall drinks above their heads.
The pedicabs joust with the motorbikes.
Street artists swim against the waves
of men in shorts and women in straw hats,
and sandals, swirling skirts. Expensive cars
display their chrome and tinted glass
and push through crowded streets.
But in the byways, beneath live oaks
and bougainvillea, the shadows gather.
Roosters scratch and root beneath the duff,
under the slash pines and the cypresses,
as if in search of keys to mysteries.
A breeze from off the Gulf portends
a storm before nightfall. The drunken
chef shouts from the back door
of the Commodore, wishing himself
back in the days of Henry Flagler
or Ernest Hemingway, dark ghosts
who gather over the Dry Tortugas,
red sundown a heartbeat's length away.

Duval Street is a downtown street in Key West, Florida. It was named for William Pope Duval, the first territorial governor of Florida.

A Motel on Key West

Outside the waves are hissing.
Look in the moldy wicker drawer
and find a hand. Look in the toilet.
See a face. The ebb tide waves,
like snakes; the marl decays beneath
the land. This island is a tomb
for countless generations. Order a drink
at Sloppy Joe's and watch the sunset.
Girls dance on the stage at Dirty Harry's.
Is it polluted water from the mainland
pours through the aqueduct at night?
Pray to be alive at dawn.

The sea, monstrous but restless

The sea, monstrous but restless
heaves against the shore, a giant
female body, writhing in its sleep
but ready to wake, devour all,
aided by winds that sweep like horses
from the south and east; a dread disease
like red tide, whose evil smell invades the land
and everyone, it seems, until the Gulf winds
sweep it all away and calm returns.

On Key West

The pier, infatuated by the ocean,
steps out boldly on her long
thin legs. The gaps between
her skinny boards reveal
the seething tide.
The waves caress her legs
as she reaches out, so tall,
so lonely, toward the gray horizon,
smiling cynically.

The cold excites, the foam arouses;
shadows play around the eddies
and the vortices that make
her see her future in a mating
with a giant wave that strips her,
leaves her standing naked
beneath the swirling sky.
Accused of carelessness and pride,
she is a creature of the land,
too eager for the depth that fools
us all by seeming what we most desire.

Sanibel

A Map

A great sea turtle swims
across the map, its mottled
shell and fins an iridescent
hue with flashes,
green, orange and blue.
Beneath the turtle, Tarpon Bay,
Captiva Island swim,
complete with roads and bridges.
Follow the shore to Knapps Point,
out, then round the island to the causeway.

A keen observer hears
the waves beat on the southern
shore. The detailed markings
conjure visions of shells
and sand and crowded
thoroughfares. Depth markings
in the Gulf will cool the heat
along the Periwinkle Way.
But still the map at best implies
the vastness stretching south
and west, with shrimp boats rolling
in the swells, the dolphins diving,
and mirages that are Naples' towers
far, far out, just at the verge of visible.

Shell-Seekers

In darkness
before sunrise
sandaled shell-seekers
search the ebb-tide,
bent along the beach
and sandbars
like worshipers
of some strange
sea-god, whose
manna comes
as crumbs
of calcium
at dawn.
As the sun comes up
and pelicans resume
their dives,
the wrinkled acolytes
return to bed
their ceremonies done.

This Island Is a State of Mind

This island is a state of mind,
from Blind Pass to the causeway,
and all the pungent pagus
in between; the mostly placid
plage; a world apart yet of a piece,
with peace descending
from the palms, palmettos,
bouganvillea, jacarandas;
hidden in hibiscus groves
and mangrove forests,
under bridges, on the beach.

February Sonnet

For Ken

Below the lofty cirrus,
cumulonimbus clouds grow fat
above the hot tub while the guests
in swim attire and designer shades
trade stories of their day. The clouds
of steam and hot air from the pool
float up to swell the clouds still more
and make the afternoon evaporate
to cocktail hour and the end of play.
The lights come on in condo porch
and parking lot. The dissipating clouds
reveal a moon and stars above
the island as the guests retell
their tales then hit the hay.

At the Club

Like boiling frogs they float, their skinny
legs drawn up, or slowly flexing
in the froth and bubbles of the hot tub.
They lounge, it seems, for hours; eyes closed,
or staring out; no effort, energy, or life.

In the locker, a missing digit, red,
swollen ankles, hammer toes, the zipper-
stitches of heart surgery: these are
the wounds of life—a war—the wear
and tear and strife. We're naked,
each body says; in the steam room
or the showers. All alike in our
mortality. No one pays attention.
This is how we are.

On Sanibel

The island's posh, and crowded, but
the beaches shine with shells,
umbrellas, and the footprints of the rich.

Marooned between the mainland and
the Gulf, we yearn for Key West
as the croc yearns for salt water;
the beauty and the tackiness,
the Sun 'n' Surf, Casa Marina and ghosts
of greats who gathered there.

On Sanibel II

Crabbers check their traps in rolling seas.
Low clouds—humidity made visible—
move west to east. Days roll on
like storms above the Gulf.

Down here we squander sunsets
thinking there's no end of them.
An osprey soars above the million-
dollar yachts and tourists wait
for open tables at Grandma Dot's.

Big winds along the beach,
the Gulf switches from green
to gray. Umbrellas flap
the sunbathers pull on their cover-ups
and birds are quiet for the day.

That Florida Feeling

I am no land's man
I pillage what I can
Without a qualm or plan.

Pelicans emerge from mist
above the beach. Others
paddle the heaving waves
near shore, heads just visible
above the sleeping/sloping sand.

The palms lean toward the beach,
dun sand reflects the light.
Pelicans skim the waves.

The palm trees lean, their
elephant feet set firmly
in the grass, their green crowns
unkempt heads of punk hair
waving in the breeze.

At noon the horizon
disappears into the sea.
The sun is hot, the water
silver-blue. The crows
and ibises, the pelicans
are listless in the heat.

On the shore, a million shells, the waste
of waves; the ibises now dance
above the lawn; the gulls
and pelicans, above the surf.

The tourists carry drinks
to watch the sun drop
into the Gulf.
They watch in vain
to see a green flash
as the red sun touches
deep blue water at
the horizon line.

Now full moon, ebb tide
and the Gulf is restless
in its bed.

Blind Pass

The road winds northwest through the palms
and bougainvillea.
The shoreline angles north.
They meet as if by chance; surprise.
A clearing, the horizon opens.
In 1969 a hurricane came
and cut a wound that never healed.
Captiva Island was born.

Today the Gulf licks daily at the wound;
the tides sweep blue green as a friend
to fill the bay, while
speedboats loll through, cars buzz
across the bridge and nearly naked girls
sunbathe beside the flow of water
past the white sand, foreskin of the island.

Pine Island / Another World

To the east is Pine Island,
cheaper, dense with foliage,
coral and development.
Cross the straits to Matlacha.
Bert's Bar & Grill.
The island lolls in mangrove forests
a fat and satiated dame,
its alligators, ibises, and pelicans,
content to breathe beneath the lychee
and the mangos, a burning Florida sun,
and, like the marsh rice rat, to mate
and propagate while osprey, herons,
egrets, spoonbills, time
and tides determine all.
Go to Bokeelia, Jug Creek Shoals
and look across the northern end
and lose yourself in Boca Grande,
palms and pines and driftwood
of the Cayo Costa. Dream.

From Lover's Key

From Lover's Key, Estero Pointe and Dog
Beach Park, to Barefoot Beach
the Gulf tide rolls and writhes.
The heat, humidity, and sand,
enough to make a grown man mad.
The babe in tiny butt-cheek bikini says
my souvenir's my tan.

The South Side

Keep going past the causeway
intersection; enter a new
dimension of this island world.
Up Yachtsman Drive you'll find
smug mansions that appear
to sneer at tourists venturing
too near. Pass Paper Fig
and take a left, you'll find
the place an old bird built—
a restaurant on a pier.
Then stare at billionaires
on the docks below,
who wash their million-dollar
yachts in cut-offs, dungarees,
while trophy brides in skimpy thongs
loll on the decks above, under the sun,
or stretch beneath the shade
of biminis as blue as any bay.

The Lure of Sanibel

Ahi, Mahi, whelks and Wahoo,
twin-tail, triple-tail, the monk
and mangrove snapper. Feast
on these, endure the spell
of Sanibel, then drive
from Blind Pass to the lighthouse
stare across Caloosahatchee
to the lights that flash
at sunset on the mainland;
watch the clouds disperse
above the bridge and bay
and feel a cool Gulf
hand across your back,
inviting you to stay.

The Way North

A Theft in Charleston

I stole the quarters from the wishing
well as evening fell. The shifting
surface in the lamplight showed my face,
twisted by greed and fear. I plunged
my arm in to the elbow. My arm
was broken by late sunlight's fading sheer.

Now my luck is running bad.
The storm clouds cluster over breakers
as the dark sea runs.
                        Black cats
follow me, and ladders lean in,
ready to betray me. Shattered mirrors
follow me; shivered reflections haunt
my nights, and salt thrown out is no protection
from the dark that lurks beyond my fears.

The Old Shrimp Shack

The old shrimp shack stands
high on piles above the estuary,
its peeling paint and sagging
roof recalling better days;

the water tank, a rusty gray,
the ladder, missing steps,
a skiff hangs half-submerged
beside a dock that leans
solicitously toward the bay.

Their livelihood was gone,
they left the place to pelicans
and sharks that swim between
the piles in search of bait or lie
in wait for unsuspecting visitors.

An Apalachicola Suite

I

Slash pines on the barrier island
cling to sand with roots
like tentacles, or black beard moss
bared by the trade winds and the hurricanes.

The dunes rise, wave-like
from the beach; the beach-grass
ripples in the breeze. The peaks of sand
grow nipples in the wind.

II

The quiet of the creek; the marsh
stands silent in its green-gold
thickness; impenetrable to sight.
Above the spears of grass a single
mast, the mystery of the estuary.
Pelicans fly low or hover
before alighting on a mooring post.

III

At low tide the sand shines in the sun,
the seabirds stand quiet in pools
as they wait for tell-tale movements
on the water around them.

Drivers on the highway bridge
see ospreys and the pelicans
dive as the gulls swing
seaward in the sun and wind.

Apalachicola Impressions

I

Few things graceful as a pelican,
skimming the Creek.

A sad little backwater town,
its only claim to fame,
its oysters, which are
thinning out.

II

A call girl leaves the Water Street Hotel,
her suitcase and her cork-heeled slip-ons
clicking on the road.
She throws the suitcase in her Lexus,
blonde ponytail waving to her John goodbye.

III

"Bite Me Deli and Catering"
Captain Ron Bloodworth,
Fishing guide and one-time pirate.

IV

From Panacea to Port St. Joe, Florida's
"forgotten coast" winds east to west,
face to the Gulf; ramshackle cottages
and Hurricane-proof mansions dot the shoreline.

Dollar Treed

Energy bars and Juicy
Fruit, cut-rate condiments
and flimsy foil; lighters,
batteries and body wash
all cheap from China.
The job sucks
life from staff
and shoppers equally.

Only the frenzied fury
to find a bargain
animates the customers
to seem life-like and staff
to feint the manners
of the walking dead.

Traveling North

Up 231 and toward the heart of Alabama:
along the road the faded signs
with dropped-off letters:
"__top 'n' Shop." Salute
the Dollar General in every town.
Folks evicted from their nickel-
dime economies move into mobile
homes or manufactured houses.

"Hurricane-Lawyer" advertises
all along the forgotten coast
of Florida. The road tends north,
to Dothen, winds past red dog roads,
ramshackle houses, abandoned filling
stations and rotting produce stands.

Home

Heading north through Alabama,
Tennessee, the Bourbon Road,
the dreams of shells are fading as
the fog becomes a snowstorm and
the freeway becomes obscured.
Returning wearied and a little tanned
but warmed by memories—
a myriad of mermaids melting
in the surf—we lug our souvenirs
and luggage past the rivers frozen
or in flood, toward a horizon
past imagining but fresh with promise
where a flame ignites renewed resolve,
a scintilla of hope—we're home.

Ed Block is Emeritus Professor of English at Marquette University, Milwaukee, WI, where he taught courses on—among others—Denise Levertov and Czeslaw Milosz and conducted workshops in creative writing.

He began publishing poetry in 1997 with a poem in *CrossCurrents*. Since then he has published over fifty poems in journals like *Plainsongs*, *Nebraska Life*, *Janus Head*, *Parabola*, *Bramble*, and *Lake Country Journal*. His collection, *Anno Domini*, appeared in 2016; *Seasons of Change* in 2017. His interviews, essays, and reviews on literary topics, have appeared in a variety of journals. He continues to write poetry, tend a garden, and enjoy retirement in Greendale, Wisconsin.

Follow the author at greendalebrushandquill.com

www.ingramcontent.com/pod-product-compliance
Lightning Source LLC
Chambersburg PA
CBHW071758040426
42446CB00012B/2614